BREATHLESS
Soul

A Collection of Poems

SANDRA ARNONE

XULON PRESS

Xulon Press
2301 Lucien Way #415
Maitland, FL 32751
407.339.4217
www.xulonpress.com

© 2021 by Sandra Arnone

All rights reserved solely by the author. The author guarantees all contents are original and do not infringe upon the legal rights of any other person or work. No part of this book may be reproduced in any form without the permission of the author.

Due to the changing nature of the Internet, if there are any web addresses, links, or URLs included in this manuscript, these may have been altered and may no longer be accessible. The views and opinions shared in this book belong solely to the author and do not necessarily reflect those of the publisher. The publisher therefore disclaims responsibility for the views or opinions expressed within the work.

Unless otherwise indicated, Scripture quotations taken from the Holy Bible, New International Version (NIV). Copyright © 1973, 1978, 1984, 2011 by Biblica, Inc.™. Used by permission. All rights reserved.

The poems in this book are works of fiction. Names, characters, places and incidents either are the product of the author's imagination or are used fictitiously. Any resemblance to actual persons, living or dead, business establishments, events or locales is entirely coincidental.

Paperback ISBN-13: 978-1-66282-658-0
Ebook ISBN-13: 978-1-66282-659-7

BREATHLESS
Soul

For my grandson,
William Anthony Arnone
2018-2020

Forever in my heart

To my readers:
Thank you for reading my poetry.

Jesus
The Alpha and the Omega

Preface

The death of my grandson brought me to a time of devastating pain. I knew deep in my soul that a very conscious decision had to be made or I could not survive. There were but two choices: I could turn away from a God who did not answer my prayers, or I could remain faithful by giving up my grief and anger to Him in prayer.

The poems that I share with you in *Breathless Soul* reflect my struggle with this unspeakable loss. Each poem represents a foot stone on the path of my journey. My hope is that in reading *Breathless Soul,* you will be *assured* that only with *God* can we face the pain of this world and remain.

Psalm 57

Have pity on me, God: have
pity on me,
for in you I take refuge.
In the shadow of your wings
I take refuge,
till harm pass by.

PART ONE
See Me

CONTENTS

Winter *3*
Love *4*
Breathless *5*
Hope *6*
Flight *7*
Fool *8*
William *9*
Joy *10*
Anchor *11*
Touched *12*

Winter

You are the flames that burn
Deep within my soul.
You ward off the inevitable winter
The season that is to come.

I embrace the winter,
As it is another road.
But I will take you with me,
Even as winter unfolds.

Eyes of a child;
Soul of the old;
Dichotomy of the spirit
Yet to unfold.

Greet me with loving arms,
Tenderly, when I come home.

Love

Take me home.
I want to be with you.
See what you see;
Love what you love.
Stay with me.
Never let them take us apart.
You are my other side,
My wholeness.
Without you, I am empty;
Lost;
An empty vessel.
Why must there be change?
Why?
I cannot bear the emptiness
This change brings.
Never to be whole again;
To cling to you;
See your smile;
Taste your love.
Alone and empty,
I will disappear.

Breathless

Who holds the key to wholeness?
What determines who is complete?
Can an armless child be held?
A breathless child, see what he or she
Was meant to see?

Who is the judge of wholeness?
Be damned! You are not the voice.
The voice is the Word, and
The Word is my God.

Only He brings the truth and light
To me.

Hope

The tears rush like a raging river,
Serving no purpose but to cleanse.

Change my rage to softness, understanding.
Save me from the evil hand.

Take my cry and send it back
On eagle's wings.

Softened, calm, and open,
Forgive the one who stumbles.
Always smile upon me.

Flight

They are without knowledge,
Determined but weak.

Their road is linear and reaches the top,
The top is to be defined in your way.

The sparrow preens, removes the devil;
Prepares the wings for flight.

Never failing carrying its spirit
On the wing.

Touch my baby boy carry him
On your wing.
Take him to heights
Where the sun warms his face
And begets an everlasting smile.

Fool

Fool that I am;
That I might understand
The road with its curves and turns.

Fool to believe that I determine and control
The stops and starts,
The beginnings and ends,
The smiles and tears.

Fool ! Can I be other than this?
I don't know.

William Anthony

The face of a cherub;
A soul shared by two.
Always by your side, never faltering
Who has had this? So pure and selfless.

You because you are so loved.
You are an endless gift.
You forever in our hearts.

Rest my angel, finally free.
Shared your heart so you will always be.

Joy

Can an unimaginable sadness
Be filled with awe?
Can there be light, even though
The sun never rose?

Can you see the face of Jesus
And hear His voice on earth?
Yes. Listen and be present in the Lord.

He waits at your door
But you must ask Him in.
Can you do this?
For here is joy.

Anchor

So many beautiful colors in your quilt;
So many beautiful faces.

Faces of love, compassion, faith.
A quilt that covers me when I'm afraid.
Wraps me in your friendship,
Never allowing the cold winds to touch me.

Who are you? So tender and steadfast.
You are my anchor;
My everything calm in this turbulent place.

Touched

You chose me.
You told me so in your small child's voice
How could that be?
I could not understand.

I cared for you unconditionally,
Never faltering;
Never sure it was enough.

You grew and, still,
I wasn't sure that it was enough.

Then you stood in front of me,
In front of God with the sun
Lighting your face.
And I knew
You were so much more than enough.

Psalm 34
I sought the Lord, and he answered me and delivered me from all my fears.

PART TWO
Hear Me

CONTENTS

Cheated *17*
Shield My Eyes *18*
Ask Too Much *19*
Grandson Mine *20*
Sometimes *21*
Selfish Me *22*

Cheated

I have a gift that won't be
Opened.
I have a love that won't be
Shared.
I have a space that can't be
Filled.
And a heart that will never
Mend.
I have an emptiness so
Deep.
A sadness, un-compared.
I have been cheated
And here is where I am.

Shield My Eyes

Beautiful little faces;
So many to see.
I say the words
Expected of me.
Hide the pain
That stabs me inside.
The knowledge that,
Little by little, I die.
I want to love the little faces
So pure and new
But they are not mine.
They belong to you.
Where are these faces
That look like me?
The ones that I pray for
But may never be.

Ask Too Much

Do not be bitter.
Do not ask why.
Hold your head up
Look toward the sky.
Forgive the selfish
For not being near.
Each has a cross
They must bear.
These words sound uplifting
But wither away
When my heart is so broken.
And there seems no way
To help me move on.
I have so much to give.
Let the sun shine
So I still want to live.

Grandson Mine

I see you , your eyes speak to me.
I say, "Why this?" You say, "Meant to be."
I say, "Too much suffering." You say, "Yes."
I say, "Please stop this." You say, "Not yet."

They say, it's too late so you tell them to see.
They say no hope. You say hope runs eternally.
They say it's done. You say it's just beginning.
You are so young and so wise.
You stayed so briefly but left an indelible mark.
You are a whisper in the ears of many,
Soothing and calm
An invitation to see,
Helping them to a place they should be
Like quiet above the constant sound.
You say, "Listen." I pray that your words will heal me somehow.

Sometimes

Sometimes it is not right.
The pieces just don't fit.
Souls just can't commit.
Sometimes we see,
But will not act.
It is too hard.
How will we get back?
Sometimes we need to push hard
Against ourselves,
Believing there is more
Than what we see right now.
Sometimes we hear a whisper
That keeps us unnerved,
Until it becomes a shout
And it must be heard.
Move on don't be afraid.
I am always with you.

Selfish Me

There is a name I wanted to hear,
From the lips of a little boy I held so dear.
The name was never uttered,
But heard with my eyes.

I know you knew me.
It was no surprise.
You are from me,
A most special part.

You're from your dad.
He is my heart.
Of course you loved me.
There is no way
That I could not know this,
Even today.
Utter my name; although you are gone,
I will hear it from afar.
Carried on a robin's wing;
Alive in the coming spring.

Tell me, again and again,
That I am grandma , your grandma.
For my love for you will never end.

Psalm 145: 15-16
The eyes of all look to you,
 and you give them their food at the proper time.
You open your hand
 and satisfy the desires of every living thing.

PART THREE
Heal Me

CONTENTS

Torn Feathers 27
Listen, Grandma 29
Help Me 30
Dad 31
Two Places 33
Tell William 35
Choose 37
There Will Be More 39
Walk With Me 40
Whispers 41
Where is Your God? 42
Where Will You Be? 44

Torn Feathers

As I spread my wings,
Soaring and watching from above,
Life is moving and changing all at once
I revel in my flight,
A view of those below.
Am I worthy of this gift?
My feathers beautiful
As they reflect the shimmering sun.
They seize the updraft of the day.
Will it always be this way?
Then a feather torn.
I recall the day
Raging tears
Will they ever go away?
Again, a feather ripped away
A gaping hole remains
I need these feathers.
They are a part of me.
How will I soar and feel so free?
Then, the smallest feather plucked so brutally;
They said it would not be so hard to lose
Fools! That was the one that best reflected me.
I can no longer take flight.

Where are the winds to carry me?
Feathers to hold me tight
I cry out though God does not answer me.
Don't make me stay down there,
For in the noise I cannot hear the voice of my heart.
Protect me, Lord.
I am so naked without these feathers.
They were once a shield for me.

Listen, Grandma

I see your tears.
They make me sad.
Grandma listen to me now
You need to know
How truly happy I am.
I feel so light and free.
There are no tubes or tethers
Anchoring me
I am running and singing
Without pain or fear.
It is unbelievably beautiful here.
Believe as I tell you
That heaven is real.
So live your life, Grandma.
Know that I am near.
I am always with you.
Never fear
God has His plan.
Please don't ask why —
God always loves you
And forever, so will I.

Help Me

I pray when the sun rises.
I pray when it sets.
The calm is short lived.
It's so hard to rest.
I can't find my place
My mind keeps drifting away
To a place where those memories
Ask me to stay.
Need to be positive;
Keep spirits high.
Nothing seems to matter.
Help me survive.
My life has been frozen.
It stopped when you died
Help me, I pray.
I need to believe
There will be a new day.

Dad

Dad, don't be sad
Please don't feel guilt.
There is no place for this.
I know how you loved me.
You were always there.
I looked to you
To know who I am
I am your boy.
Your son, so proud
To have had you
Such an extraordinary dad.
You are so right
We will laugh and play.
But until then
God expects you to stay
Strong and steadfast;
To share your gifts.
You were born for this
To lift the spirits of others
And show them the way
To love without boundaries.
You do this each day
You are my dad,

The best part of me.
We are father and son,
This will forever be.

Two Places

I live in two places.
Since you've been gone,
I live in this world
And the one beyond.
We talk each day.
I hear your voice.
It keeps me steady.
You are now breathless,
But not like before
You are breathless because
Of the world you explore:
Running, jumping, and living God's dream
It must be so beautiful
I wish I could be with you
To share in all this
So I live in my mind, trying to see
What your world is like now
And how sweet it must be
I read about heaven;
Those who arrived
But were made to come back
To this world in this time.
You are with me today.

And I look for your signs:
A sudden breeze, a note from my wind chime
I know it is you, my precious boy.
Never stop reaching out to your grandma.
Your grandma I will always be.

Tell William

The sun rose over the mountain
I woke up to see
That spring was inevitable.
I wish you were here with me.

The earth is a stage
For new life to perform.
Soft green seedlings and insects abound;
I touch the ground gently
So I can push away leaves.
It is so amazing what lies beneath.

If you were with me,
I would explain
How the winter protected this new life
And let it sleep until today.

I would take you by the hand
And show you the way that birds share their song;
And plan for the day
That new life will emerge
From a nest so designed
To keep predators at bay,

Until their fledglings can fly.

New life, William on this spring day
I miss you so terribly.
Nothing will take my sadness away.

Choose

What should I choose?
Listen to me
I can be angry and hopeless.
I have every right to be
I carry a sadness.
Why should it be?
There are others who harvest
The seeds that they've sown.
My seeds are as fine
I wanted my grandson to live,
So I could share what I know
About life and God's gifts.
Why shouldn't it be so?
I am so angry!
You would be too.
Then my mind stops
And my heart takes control.
I know how to choose.
For they tell me so
Those I have lost
Shout out loud and clear
"Don't be sad you know that we're here
To counsel you

Choose what you know
Is the right path to take.
We are all with you,
Make no mistake
Your harvest is great.
Don't fail to see
All the gifts He has given you.
Let your heart lead.
That is where your wisdom lies
God's plan is written.
You will one day realize
That His love is real.
He wants only your happiness,
Even when you cannot see beyond today."

There Will Be More

I've allowed myself time
To feel the pain;
To question why.
My constant refrain;
It is time to believe
What I know to be true
There is a time for grieving;
A time to see things through
God is my support.
I ask that He be patient with me.
Even when I falter,
In my heart I know
He knows me.

Walk With Me

He came to the mountain,
Arrived in the spring
Like a bright, burning star
Filled with fervor and vision.
Of what tomorrow could be
He said, "Walk with me
Leave your sadness behind.
It has no purpose in this time.
Seize your happiness and pursue your dreams.
Leave the hurtful behind
Witness what positivity can do,
A change of perspective is all you need;
You know this to be true."
So I walked with him.
In my heart, I held his hand,
Afraid to let him know how much I depended on him,
Not wanting to burden or tie him down.
We walked and my dimmed spirit ignited.
The cold dark days behind,
Sadness releasing me after so long a time.
New dreams viable now
He is the best part of me.
The passionate pursuer of truth and integrity,
I hope he will always say
"Walk with me."

Whispers

A tickle for my ear;
Thoughts for me to ponder.
What is this little voice?
Always in the background;
Not an annoyance just a whisper.
Who whispers to me?
Do you have a name?
Do you know me?
A tickle for my brain
You make me smile, make me cry,
Make me reach out sometimes
Where would I be without these whispers?
Dark and locked-up inside
Many years, much living behind,
You've never left my mind
Take me to that place you know
The one I can't escape
 A time of youth
Now so far away.
Where are you?
Promise me you'll stay. Whispers...

Where is Your God?

"There is no God," they say to me.
"Your grandson died.
Where was God's tender mercy?
You are a romantic fool!
There is no entity;
Just an untamed cosmic, cacophony
Talk of love and hope,
Where have you been?
See the hatred and violence from within.
Where's the God you pray to each day?
You're a fool!
He left now make your way
Like the rest of us today
You're on your own admit it!
Would a God allow this mess?
The death and violence;
You know it's true
What I say should make much sense to you
But you are a fool,
As I said before
Until you see
I will say no more."
I have seen

It is the face of *Jesus*.
This is why I cry out to you
An invitation to see the truth.
It is man who chooses to stand without his God.
This is the evil.
Can you turn your rage to understanding?
Choose love before hate?
Open the door and come in;
He waits for you.
Seek the love of *Jesus*.
You will be different than before
And then, you will know
That I am not a fool at all.

Where Will You Be?

The cold winds have arrived.
I have covered my garden with blankets of nature's confetti.
The golden leaves reflect the late day sun
And the brightest reds, my heart
That belongs to you.

I woke to see the full moon create a luminous light
Upon the pines;
Their shadows strong against the ground.
My mind says, "sleep,"
But my childlike heart refuses.
My eyes will not close to this incredible sight,
For how many more will I be allowed?

I call out to you in my heart
Where will I find you now?
We would meet in my garden.
The gentlest breeze would carry your impish smile to me.
You would observe my hands, dirty and wet.
The sweet notes from my wind chime would summon a smile to my face.

Now I am afraid, as the garden will be dormant.
Where will we meet each day?
I won't survive until spring.

Author's Page

Sandra (Sandi) Arnone is an elementary school teacher. She received a B.A. degree in English and an elementary teacher certification. Her M.S. degree is in early childhood education. Teaching has, and always will be, her passion.

Sandi is an avid reader, wordsmith, and lover of canines, large and small. Brutus, her Pembroke Welsh Corgi "extraordinaire," has been her constant companion for nearly fourteen years. Sandi enjoys hiking, listening to music, and sharing her dinner table with her wonderful family and incredible friends. She lives in upstate New York on eighteen acres of heaven on earth.

Psalm 18:19
He brought me into this spacious place
He rescued me because he delighted in me.

I want to thank you, Mom, for showing me how to be a strong woman and teaching me how to love; and to my girlfriends in *faith*, especially my dearest Denise, for walking beside me in my journey.

CPSIA information can be obtained
at www.ICGtesting.com
Printed in the USA
BVHW082332070921
616209BV00008B/214